What on Earth? Life in the Tundra

What on Earth?

Brrrrrrr its cold!

crack!

What is this
walrus doing?
Turn this page for the answer.

First published in 2005 by
Book House an imprint of
The Salariya Book Company
25 Marlborough Place
Brighton
BN1 1UB

HB ISBN 1-905087-41-1
PB ISBN 1-905087-42-X

Visit our website at **www.book-house.co.uk**
for free electronic versions of:
You Wouldn't Want to be an Egyptian Mummy!
You Wouldn't Want to be a Roman Gladiator!
Avoid joining Shackleton's Polar Expedition!
Avoid Sailing on a 19th-Century Whaling Ship!

Due to the changing nature of internet links, The Salariya Book Company
has developed an online list of websites related to the subject of this book.
This site is updated regularly. Please use this link to access the list:
http://www.book-house.co.uk/WOE/tundra

A catalogue record for this book is available from the British Library.

Printed and bound in China.

Editors:	Ronald Coleman
	Sophie Izod
Senior Art Editor:	Carolyn Franklin
DTP Designer:	Mark Williams

Picture Credits Julian Baker: 8, 9, 11, Elizabeth Branch: 1,
2, 24, John Francis: 6, 7, B and C Alexander, NHPA: 22, 23,
27, T. Kitchin and V Hurst, NHPA: 26, Genny Anderson: 17,
NASA: 26(r), Corel: 3, 8, 9, 10, 11, 13, 14, 15, 16, 18, 20,
21, 30, 31, John Foxx: 19, Corbis: 25, PhotoDisc: 28, 29

What on Earth?

Making an airhole!

A walrus uses its tusks to
make a hole up through the
ice to breathe. Its tusks can
grow up to one metre (three
feet) long.

What on Earth? life in the Tundra

PENNY CLARKE

A change of colour?

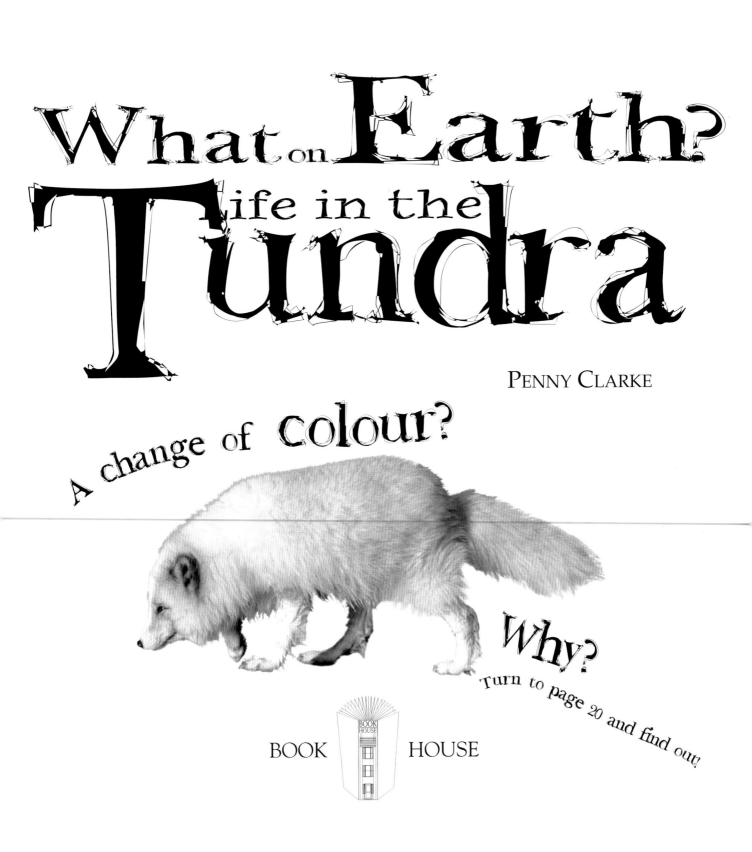

Why?

Turn to page 20 and find out!

BOOK HOUSE

Contents

Introduction   5

What is the tundra?   6

Where is the tundra?   8

Why is it so cold?   10

What is the Aurora Borealis?   12

Can anything live on the tundra?   14

How do plants survive?   16

Can birds survive in the tundra?   18

What about mammals?   20

Do people live in the tundra?   22

Does the tundra change?   24

What is the tundra like now?   26

How would you survive in the tundra?   27

Tundra facts   28

Glossary   29

What do you know about the tundra?   30

Index   32

What on Earth?

Non-stop flight!

Bar-tailed godwits are birds that make the longest non-stop migration. They fly over 9,656 kilometres (6,000 miles) from Alaska to Australia in just five or six days.

Introduction

The tundra is land adjoining the Arctic Ocean. It is one of the coldest and **bleakest** regions on earth. The winters are very long and very cold, and the summers are very short and only slightly less cold. Life is very hard for the plants, animals and people who make it their home. They have had to adapt to cope with the extreme cold and the biting winds which whip across the tundra all year long.

Where does the word 'tundra' come from?

The word 'tundra' comes from the Sami language and means a **'treeless plain'**. It was first used by the nomadic Sami people of northern Scandinavia to describe the cold plains where their herds of reindeer grazed in summer.

How cold is it?

The average temperature is -28°C (-18°F) which is more than chilly, but it's still not the coldest place on Earth. The coldest temperature ever recorded was -89°C (-129°F) in Antarctica near the South Pole.

What is the tundra?

The word 'tundra' describes vast, cold, treeless plains on lands which lie just south of the North Pole. The tundra has long cold winters. A blanket of snow covers the region and the soil is **frozen hard**. Even in summer, frost is common.

The sun hardly rises above the horizon, so winter days have only one or two hours of daylight. Summers last just a few months, but the sun never really sets, so the region is called the land of the midnight sun'.

Willow grouse

Caribou

Red-backed vole

White-tailed sea eagle

Wolves work as a team to separate
a musk ox calf from the herd.

Herd of musk oxen

Wolves

Musk ox calf

Lichen

where is the tundra?

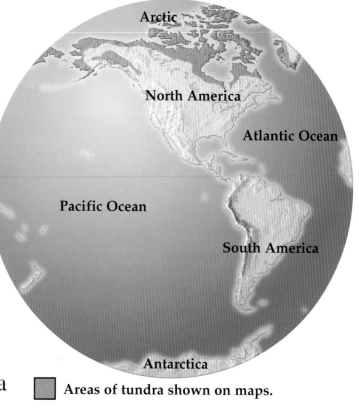

Tundra regions are only found in the northern hemisphere, close to the Arctic Circle. The most northerly points of North America, Europe and Asia all have areas of tundra. In the Southern hemisphere, no land lies close to the frozen continent of Antarctica, so tundra conditions do not exist there.

Areas of tundra shown on maps.

Does the climate of the tundra vary?

The climate of the tundra varies little across North America, northern Europe and Asia, so the plants and animals are similar throughout the region. Wolves and Arctic foxes range far north over the tundra in summer.

Polar bears like the cold...

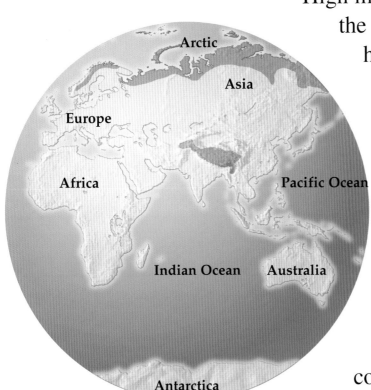

High mountains like the Andes, the Alps and the Himalayas have areas where the climate and vegetation are rather like the Arctic tundra. Scientists call these areas 'alpine tundra' to show they are **different**. The main difference is the length of the seasons. Regions of alpine tundra are very cold, but their winters are shorter and summers longer than those of the Arctic tundra.

What happens when winter sets in?

...so they go north in winter!

As winter sets in, the wolves and foxes move southward to follow their prey. They continue to hunt birds like the willow grouse, and animals like reindeer. Willow grouse do not migrate like so many of the birds that nest on the tundra each summer. Today, musk oxen are found only on the tundra of North America and Greenland.

Why is it so cold?

When the sun shines directly overhead it is at its hottest. But the sun is never directly over the tundra so it never gets hot there, even in summer. As the Earth travels around the sun, the tundra is always tilted away from the sun's warmth.

How tall is a musk oxen?

Male musk oxen can be 1.5 metres (5 feet) tall at shoulder height. Musk oxen are the only large mammals that can survive on the tundra.

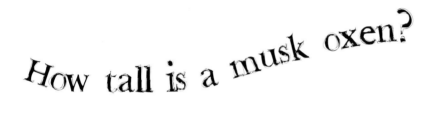

Why does it stay cool?

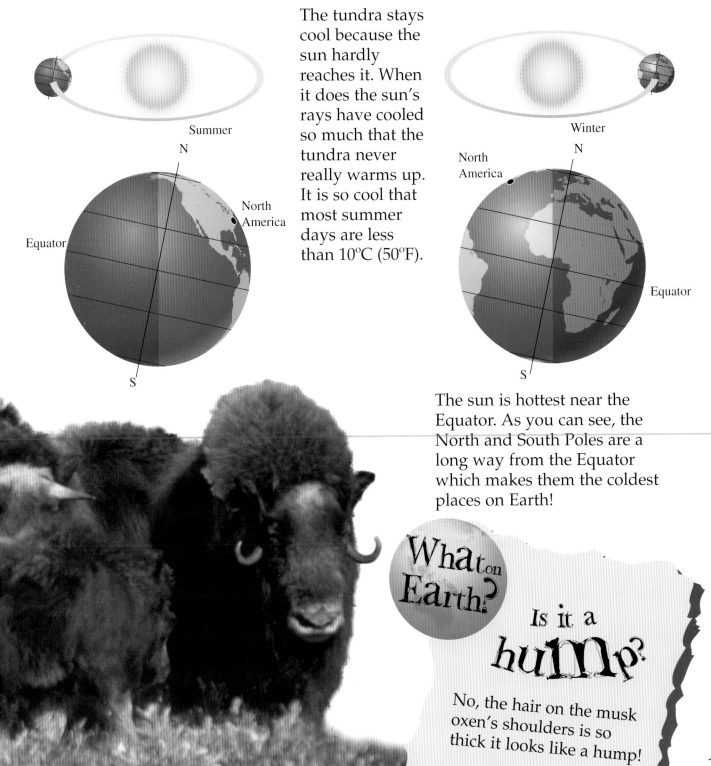

Summer

N

Equator

North America

S

Winter

N

North America

Equator

S

The tundra stays cool because the sun hardly reaches it. When it does the sun's rays have cooled so much that the tundra never really warms up. It is so cool that most summer days are less than 10°C (50°F).

The sun is hottest near the Equator. As you can see, the North and South Poles are a long way from the Equator which makes them the coldest places on Earth!

What on Earth?

Is it a hump?

No, the hair on the musk oxen's shoulders is so thick it looks like a hump!

11

What is the Aurora Borealis?

In winter, spectacular coloured lights fill the sky over the tundra. Called the 'Aurora Borealis' or 'Northern Lights', this fantastic natural display may only last for a few minutes, and then it vanishes. In past times the lights gave rise to myths about gods and monsters - 'Aurora' was the Romans' goddess of dawn and 'Borealis' the Greeks' god of the north wind.

What causes them?

Gigantic explosions (flares) on the sun's surface thrust tiny particles out into space at speeds of about 161 km (100 miles) a second. They reach the Earth around 24 hours later. As they travel down into the Earth's atmosphere, they collide with particles in the air. It is these collisions that cause light.

What colours?

These collisions take place at different heights in the Earth's atmosphere. The height of each collision creates a different colour. The Aurora Borealis makes purple, blue, green and bright red lights that flicker across the dark sky.

How powerful are they?

The lights have more electrical power than anything else in the world. They can cause powercuts and problems with satellites up in space.

What on Earth?

The Earth's burning rim?

The Vikings believed the Aurora was the Earth's burning rim. The Inuits said the lights were caused when human people met sky people.

Can anything live on the tundra?

A number of living things have adapted to the harsh conditions on the tundra. They must withstand the **biting winds** that sweep across it. They must cope with long winters, with little daylight and very low temperatures. Even in the short summers only the top surface of soil thaws, the soil below stays frozen hard. As a result the melted snow cannot drain away. This makes the ground very **boggy** and an excellent breeding ground for insects. An explosion of blackfly and mosquitoes appear in huge buzzing clouds in summer.

What's special about reindeers' hooves?

Reindeer have big hooves that splay out, giving the animal a better grip as it moves across the snow. The reindeer also use them to dig down to find plants buried in the snow.

It must be winter!

In winter the Arctic fox grows a very thick white coat. This disguises it and also protects it from the cold. As a result it can curl up on the snow and sleep even in temperatures well below freezing.

What on Earth?

Too cold for cold-blooded animals?

The tundra is too cold for cold-blooded animals like snakes and frogs. They need warmth to be able to move, breathe or feed.

How do plants survive?

It is too cold and windy for trees to grow in the tundra. Most plants there grow close to the ground to shelter from the icy winds. Lichens, mosses and small cushion-shaped flowers are most common. The cushion shape helps prevent the plant from freezing.

What on Earth?

small but very old!

Lichens grow very slowly and some types can live for up to 4,000 years!

Lichens (opposite) are very small and only grow where there is very little pollution. They have spores instead of seeds.

Survival against all odds?

As well as the cold and wind, plants on the tundra plains have to overcome shallow, poor soils and low rain fall. But on the mountains conditions are even worse.

Lichen growing on a stone

Can birds survive in the tundra?

Birds migrate to the tundra in the summer where they nest and breed. The rich supply of insects they feed on will die out as winter approaches. The birds migrate again before snow and ice returns to cover the tundra. Many birds fly south to winter in warmer places, often travelling **huge** distances.

Do all birds migrate?

Most birds migrate to avoid winter on the tundra. But the willow grouse and the eagle only migrate as far as the taiga forests, south of the tundra.

Eagle

Willow grouse

What is the taiga?

Taiga is the Russian term for the huge belt of conifer forests south of the tundra.

Night-time hunter?

Snowy owls (left) hunt in the daytime as well as at night, which is very rare. In summer snowy owls hunt small animals over the tundra, but they winter in the forest.

What on Earth?

silent and deadly?

Most birds' feathers make some noise as they fly through the air. The fluffy edges of an owl's feathers soften any noise so it can **swoop** unheard on its prey.

Whooshsssss!

What about mammals?

Mammals are warm blooded animals. This means they do not rely on the temperature of the air for warmth. Twenty-three species of **mammal** including wolves, foxes, reindeer, hares and lemmings can be found on the tundra. Polar bears have adapted so well to the cold that in winter they go further north, far out onto the **frozen** Arctic Ocean to catch seals through the ice.

A change of coat?

Arctic hare

The Arctic hare's coat also turns white in winter. This helps it to hide from foxes.

Arctic fox

Two coats?

When the Arctic fox prowls the tundra in summer, its coat is brown. This helps it blend in better to hunt its prey. As winter approaches its coat begins to change. By the time the tundra is snow-covered the fox's coat is very thick and white. It will stay like this until spring.

Yum yum!

Mice and lemmings are fast breeders but when food is scarce they have much fewer young. So Arctic foxes and snowy owls, who feed on them, go hungry.

Follow the herd?

In summer, wolves hunt herds of elk, reindeer and musk oxen that graze on the tundra. As winter approaches and the herds retreat to the forests, the wolves follow, too.

Do people live in the tundra?

Yes, despite the bitter cold, people do live in the tundra. The first people there probably followed herds of reindeer as they moved onto the tundra to graze in summer. Life is **hard**, but there is plenty of food in summer: fish, meat and birds' eggs. Meat and fish are also preserved for the winter. Animal furs provide warm clothing.

Wolf to dog?

According to legend the first sled dogs were bred from captured wolves. Throughout the tundra the people living there have their own dog breeds: huskies in Siberia, malamutes in Alaska and the Canadian Eskimo dog.

Dog to snowmobile!

Sleds pulled by teams of dogs used to be the best way to travel across the frozen tundra. Each dog had its place in the team, with the strongest as the leader.

Today snowmobiles have replaced dog sleds as the best way to cross frozen, snow-covered ground.

Where do the Sami live?

Nomadic tribes called the Sami graze reindeer on the tundra. The Sami have lived in Lapland in northern Scandinavia for thousands of years.

What on Earth?

Eat your greens!

Apart from plant shoots in spring and berries in autumn, the people of the tundra eat little fruit or vegetables - but are still healthy!

Does the tundra Change?

The Earth has existed for billions of years. During this time its climate has changed - and continues to change. At times the Earth has been much warmer, or colder than we now know. In very cold periods, called ice ages, ice covered northern Europe and North America. Beyond these huge areas of ice, the tundra stretched much further south than it does today.

When was the last ice age?

The last ice age ended about 10,000 years ago. At its peak, ice sheets over 1.6 kilometres (1 mile) thick covered half of North America. Brrr!

Where did woolly mammoths live?

Fossils (remains of very ancient living things) show how the climate has changed. Fossils of woolly mammoths, deer, bears and other tundra animals have been found as far south as London and Paris.

Hairy raincoat!

The polar bear, the largest of all bears is well equipped for the Arctic. Its thick fur coat keeps it warm and is water-repellent, too!

What is the tundra like now?

Changes to Earth's climate are felt everywhere. Global warming is partly due to pollution and the burning of fossil fuels far to the south of the tundra. This makes the tundra winters shorter and less cold. As its summers are longer, more of the permafrost (the ground that never thaws) is now thawing.

What effect is man having?

The huge open spaces of the tundra where few people live seemed ideal for building oil pipelines. But as more of the permafrost thaws, the ground supporting the pipelines becomes unstable. It shifts and cracks unevenly which might crack the pipes and cause oil to flood out.

What on Earth?

What is global warming?

Methane gas is believed to be a major cause of global warming. The tundra contains more methane than anywhere else. As the tundra thaws, methane is released into the atmosphere. The ozone layer which protects us from most of the sun's harmful ultraviolet rays, is damaged by it.

Satellite photograph of Earth and its ozone layer.

How would you survive in the tundra?

Although the tundra is home to polar bears and wolves, you are more likely to die of the cold than to be eaten by an animal. Be prepared if you travel across the tundra because if you get lost and can't catch any food there isn't much to eat apart from a tasty diet of **reindeer moss!**

Tundra Dangers

Polar bears prefer to eat seals and only attack humans if they are provoked. If a bear approaches - **don't run** as the bear can run faster than you.

Wolves are usually afraid of humans but will attack if they have a disease called 'rabies'. Use an alarm to frighten the wolves away.

Hypothermia is when you get so cold that your body temperature drops dangerously low. Try to get out of the cold and light a fire, but do not heat up again too quickly as **you could go into shock!**

What to take Check-list

Be sure to wear **mittens, hats and thick socks** to stop you getting frostbite. Make sure you take **snow shoes** so you don't fall through the ice. Don't get lost - be sure to take a **compass.** Take a good pair of warm **boots** and a **box of matches** to light a fire at night for warmth. Take an **alarm** to scare off attacking wolves and be certain to take a **two-way radio** to call for help. Learn to build an igloo or remember to take a strong **tent** and a **sleeping bag** or you will freeze. Take freeze-dried food with you as it doesn't go bad.

The narwhal is a strange looking whale. It has a large tooth growing through its upper lip to form a tusk. In the Middle Ages its tusk was thought to be a unicorn's horn.

Unicorn horn?

Narwhal

Tundra facts

The tundra is very cold because it is dry. This is because there is 10 times more moisture in rain than there is in snow.

Even though its fur is white, the skin of a Polar bear is actually black like its nose!

Small mammals, like lemmings build their nests under the snow and dig tunnels through it to search out food. By staying under the snow they shelter from the icy winds above.

Arctic terns migrate 35,405 kilometres (22,000 miles) between the North and South poles. After 7 years of migrating, they will have flown as far as the distance between the Earth and the Moon.

In the northern hemisphere 22 per cent of the land is permafrost. That's almost a quarter.

The Alaskan oil pipeline was built across a reindeer migration route, but in some places the pipes are above ground so the reindeer can pass underneath. Mind your antlers!

Moose

Glossary

Caribou North American name for the European reindeer.

Cold-blooded Term describing animals whose body temperature varies according to the temperature of the air around them.

Equator Imaginary line around the Earth's widest part.

Fossil Remains of plants and animals that lived in past ages found in rocks or dug from the ground.

Mammal Animal which is fed on its mother's milk while it is a baby.

Methane Colourless gas which doesn't smell and burns easily.

Migrate/migration Long journey made by some birds and animals in search of food and warmth.

Permafrost Ground that is always frozen.

Satellite A space technology system which orbits a planet.

Species Group of plants or animals that look alike and behave in the same way.

Woolly mammoths Creatures that lived about 10,000 years ago.

Puffin

What do you **know** about the tundra?

1 What does the word 'tundra' mean in the Sami language?

2 What is special about reindeer's hooves?

3 Why are plants very small in the tundra?

4 Why do insects breed so well after the snow melts?

5 Why is the tundra never warm?

6 Does the willow grouse migrate?

7 Have polar bears adapted to the cold?

8 What replaced sleds and dog teams in the tundra?

9 What is methane gas thought to cause?

10 Where do bar-tailed godwits migrate to in winter?

Go to page for 32 for the answer!

Can you guess how much a grizzly bear weighs?

Grizzly bears are
ranging further
north as the
climate becomes
warmer.

Index

Pictures are shown in **bold** type.

alpine tundra 9
Antarctica 5, 8
Arctic Ocean 5, 20
Arctic tundra 9
Asia 8
Aurora Borealis 12, **13**

bar-tailed godwits 4, 30

caribou **6**, 29
climate 8, 24, 26
cold-blooded 15, 29

dogs 22, 30

eagles **7**, **18**
Europe 8, 24
elk 21
Equator 11, 29

lemming 28
lichen **7**, 16, **17**
fossil 24, 26, 29
fox **3**, 8, 9, **15**, **20**, **21**

global warming 26, 32
Greenland 9
grouse **6**, 9, **18**, 30
grizzly bear **31**, 32
hare **20**
hypothermia 27

ice age 24
insect 14, 30
Inuit 13

mammal 20, 29

mammoth **24**, 29
methane 26, 29, 30
mice 21
migrate 9, 18, 29
moss 16, 27
moose **28**

mountain 9
musk ox **7**, 9, **10**, **11**, 21

narwhal **27**
nomad 23
North America 8, 9, 24
Northern Lights 12
North Pole 6, 11

oil 26
owl **19**, 21
ozone **26**

permafrost 26, 29
plants 16, 30
polar bear **8**, **9**, **25**, 27, 28, 30, 32
pollution 16
puffin **29**

reindeer 9, 14, 21, 22, 23, 30, 32

Sami **5**, 23, 30
satellite 13, 29

Scandinavia 5, 23
seal 20
sled 22, 30
soil 14, 17
South Pole 5, 11
snowmobile **22**, 32

taiga 18, 32

Viking 13
vole **6**

walrus **1**, **2**
wolf **7**, 8, 9, 20, 21, 22, 27

Answers

1 Treeless plain. (See page 5)
2 Reindeers' hooves splay out to grip the snow better. (See page 14)
3 This helps them shelter from the icy winds. (See page 16)
4 The melted snow makes the ground boggy. (See page 14)
5 The sun hardly reaches the tundra. (See page 11)
6 Only as far south as the taiga forests. (See page 18)
7 Yes, polar bears go further north in the winter. (See page 20)
8 Snowmobiles. (See page 22)
9 Global warming. (See page 26)
10 Australia. (See contents page)

An adult grizzly bear weighs up to 522kg (1150 pounds). That's the weight of nine and a half washing machines!